THE
STONECUTTER'S
HAND

Also by Richard Tillinghast:

Sleep Watch

The Knife and Other Poems

Sewanee in Ruins

Our Flag Was Still There

THE
STONECUTTER'S
HAND

POEMS BY
Richard Tillinghast

Richard Tillinghast

David R. Godine : Publisher
BOSTON

First published in 1995 by
David R. Godine, Publisher, Inc.
P.O. Box 9103
Lincoln, Massachusetts 01773

Library of Congress Cataloging-in-Publication Data

Tillinghast, Richard.
The stonecutter's hand : poems /
by Richard Tillinghast. --1st ed.
p.   cm.
I. Title.
PS3570.I38576 1994
811:54—DC20
ISBN 1-56792-0011-X

First edition
Printed in the United States of America

Acknowledgment is made to the editors of the following publications, in which some of the poems in this book originally appeared:

The Atlantic Monthly:
"Table"

The Best American Poetry 1992:
"Anatolian Journey"

Boulevard:
"The Adirondack"

Bread Loaf Anthology of Contemporary American Poetry:
"Firstness," "Savannah, Sleepless"

Cumberland Poetry Review:
"First Morning Home Again"

Gettysburg Review:
"Osman's Dream," "Sighted in Belgrade"

Harvard Magazine:
"Rhyme"

Harvard Review:
"On a Gothic Ivory"

Hudson Review:
"The Winter Funerals"

Madison Review:
"Passage"

The Nation:
"Afternoon at Griffin's"

The New Criterion:
"Manhattan, Deconstructing," "The Way the Petals Fell"

New England Review:
"A Backward Glance at Galway," "The Night of Displacement,"
"Southbound Pullman, 1945," "Xiphias"

New Virginia Review:
"Allen's Station: They," "Camp Shadywillow"

The New Yorker:
"Anatolian Journey"

The Paris Review:
"Aubade"

Ploughshares:
"House with Children," "Twos"

Sewanee Review:
"Convergence," "An Elegist's Tour of Dublin,"
"Rhymes on the Feast of Stephen"

Shenandoah:
"A Quiet Pint in Kinvara"

Southern California Anthology:
"Pasha's Daughter, 1914"

Southern Poetry Review:
"A History of Windows"

Southern Review:
"Abbey Hill," "The Ornament"

Southwest Review:
"Five Sketches, Winter," "Two Sketches, Summer"

"Pasha's Daughter, 1914" won the
1993 Ann Stanford Poetry Prize.

The author wishes to express his gratitude to the estate of Amy
Lowell for the 1990-91 Amy Lowell Travelling Fellowship in
Ireland; to the British Council for travel grants to Northern
Ireland in 1993 and 1994; to the University of Michigan for a
Faculty Recognition Award as well as support from the Rackham
School of Graduate Studies; to the American Research Institute
in Turkey for a fellowship to the University of the Bosphorus in
1990; to the Michigan Council for the Arts; to the Millay
Colony of the Arts; and to Yaddo.

Contents

THE
STONECUTTER'S
HAND

Anatolian Journey

Impedimenta of the self
Left behind somewhere, or traded
For a bag with good straps, a book of Turkish proverbs,
Sandals of proven leather,
A bottle of water called, yes, "Life"
In the language of the country — pine trees
                stencilled on the glass.

Last Thursday you were standing by a puddle
                in Istanbul asking a question:
"Why am I not home, where I should be?"
Now you're east into Asia, hearing absently
                alien conjugations,
Hoping this bus won't dizzy off this mountain.

          "So you think you're a fish now?"
           "It's true that time is a river."
From dreaming fingers your rings dumbly witness your travels.
One hand goes to your wallet, where sober dollars
              stiffly face the gaudy local bills.
Your passport is there as well,
              establishing your identity.

          Nod, and in the morning wake to
Acres of sunflowers
              warmer than any human welcome;
Haystacks domed like the domes of whitewashed mosques,
          And the Black Sea rising out of itself
              like the fragrance of remoteness.

Manhattan, Deconstructing

I walk west with a suitcase on 81st
Where among taxis the blacktop crests
At the broad opening of Park. In the unbuilt sky
Overhead, unfamiliar birdsong — seagulls
Blown inland off Atlantic squalls.
Underfoot, the controlled thunder of the IRT.

Wasn't 81st a trail once, dusty from Easter
To autumn? Draught horses watered at troughs here
And dragged tons of fish and salt through mud uphill
Over decades of winters — before the oaks were cut
For lumber and firewood, the streams made straight
And channeled underground; before the topsoil

Had the breath bricked out of it, and purple loosestrife
Flaring in ditches was crushed under asphalt.
Hillsides upstate alloyed into steel; cement
Hardened; storey above storey the city rose.
Uniformed like admirals, unfurling umbrellas,
Doormen appear now, eyeing the firmament.

That repercussion I hear as I step out
To claim a cab — that descending note
Across the black keys of the air — is that the approaching
Storm's flourish, or something new being demolished
As the city grows? Or is it an oblivious
Left-handed bass-run played before some open

Window? As I look up to divine its source,
A raindrop strikes me square in the face.
My airport taxi accelerates me out of town,
Slipping through traffic's congestive confluence,
Through the chord, the discordant concordance
Of Manhattan — built-up, weighed-down, put-upon.

Xiphias

The fish, the swordfish, *Xiphias gladius* in
Latin, swam deeply in the aquamarine —
Three hundred pounds of nerve, sleek and masterful
In his element.
Our table up the cliff shelved over the scene.

Swordfish was the *plat du jour* that day.
The cook there rubbed it with sea salt,
Garlic, crushed pepper, lemon from the lemon tree,
Kegged olive oil and thyme —
Then grilled it over local hardwood.
It was the best I've ever had.

The ocean depths were the zenith blue
Of our rented Fiat cinquecento.
A schooner skimmed over the lithe warrior in the water.
The harpoonist stretched out shirtless on the bowsprit,
His body one muscle, his arm a coiled rope.

That was before I understood about love.
I knew it would draw me into town over moonlit roads
To spend all my change on one song.
That it would keep me awake all night
And improve how the whippoorwill sang.

I wouldn't have cared if I had driven the Fiat
Off the cliff, so long as we went over together.
You were twenty-two then,
Signorina, in the South of Italy,
and I wished I had packed a gun.

The long shadow swiftly blurred.
The spotter in the crow's nest softly called
In soft Calabrian consonants the lovely word
For fish, which just then thrashed into a school of chub
And filleted a couple of dozen with his sword.

The harpoonist struck.
The three-yard pine shaft blew out for itself a tunnel
Of bubbles and disturbance.
And the blade that fishermen call a "lily"
Jabbed in just behind the gills.

The swordfish spasmed his long body-muscle,
Charged the little dory they had set out,
Stove out a plank or two just above waterline,
And then with the toothed sword jammed in up to his eyes,
The swordfish died.

That fish was lucky. He died there and then.
Pesce spada in Italian.
They lashed the carcass to the schooner,
Tied the wounded dory on behind,
And sailed into harbor.

Savannah, Sleepless

A bell has rung twelve times.
A bell has rung once.
Twice.

Could I be the last non-sleeper in Savannah?
Elevators have been upgathered

and then, with me in one, sent down again
to where duels and steam locomotives
hang on the baize walls.
Billiard balls stand expectantly,
in their round way.

Two people begin to become musical.
Powder-puff, honey-dark skin, pink gown with springy straps,
she can kiss a passing cheek and keep singing.
He tickles the ivories and looks like Nat "King" Cole.
A machine plays the beat for their song.

Two men discuss two women.
Chairs are drawn up.
Names are given.
A notebook sits apart,
entranced by the yin-yang of brandy and cigar.

No, evidently, I am not the last waking human
in the Hilton Hotel.
The singer is explaining she doesn't want
to set the world on fire,
she just wants to start a flame in the heart
of some unspecified "you."

Outside, the million tongues of the city sleep,
and the blue Atlantic draws a breath.

The Adirondack

A nimbus of attention surrounded her
In Grand Central, on the upper concourse at the bar
Where she looked for me overlooking the Great Hall:
    A brightness in that dingy marble grandeur.
    An architecture of dust and sunlight
    Fell from the windows on 42nd Street.
A brooch, antique, held her slub-silk blouse in thrall.
The ceiling curved into constellated summer skies
Pompeian green like her country house weekend eyes.

    The summer had been lunches and glances,
Involved afternoons, keys and sudden kisses.
Our train, the Adirondack, sniffing coolness up the track,
    Sensing greenness and a breezy exhalation
    Of mountain coves, left New York in the station,
    Burrowed, and surfaced to blind windows and burnt brick,
A scuffed football launched into emptiness. Then the Hudson:
Brimming, expansive, forbidding, scaled to its city.
A yacht cut the putty waves. The train blew a diesel spondee.

    September trackside sumac flared
And faded. Westchester slipped by. The Adirondack rattled
Through river towns, past a marsh where swans glided
    And willows trailed fingers in a millpond.
    Our settled flesh touched, hands paired.
    The valley broadened, air chilled, the city receded.
Her green eyes russeted. It was the last weekend
Of the season—that much was clear in our lives.
In Rhinebeck our bike tires crushed the first perished leaves.

Aubade

Steam in the pipes.
Birdsong muted.
A prowl of cat.
Ivy on a wall, the breeze layering it,
seen through Venetians.
An arm thrown over the
edge of the bed.

A stocking, a twisted undergarment, shoes.
Empty matchbooks, full ashtrays,
fume of brandy over a glass.

She gets that last twenty
minutes of sleep she likes.
He runs a razor over his jaw,
looking into the steamed mirror in a daze.

Luggage placed by a door.
Some keys on a Queen Anne table.

Sighted in Belgrade

What was that blurred candle-shimmer
I half glimpsed as I craned up from a black taxi
Rattling over cobbles, the night the king and queen
Were shot a hundred years back,
Their bodies dumped off a balcony
Into the palace garden?

High up, a Venetian chandelier
Burning 40-watt bulbs — or candles would it have been? —
Reflected in an Empire mirror with a gilt-wood frame,
The mirror in need of resilvering.
Stripes of discoloration darkening it,
Massive mahogany gloom.

And didn't they have to hack the king's
Fingers off with their swords when they murdered him —
That putty man with no strength except in his hands,
Clutching with his life's final spasm
At the railing as his body tumbled over
Into roses the Turks had planted?

Shatter of crystal smashed, and then
At the window two grey heads, like enough
To be brother and sister — the woman shrieking in Slavic
About treachery, the brother stiff
And tacit in Austrian uniform.
Then my cab lurched forward in traffic.

A Quiet Pint in Kinvara

for Jeff O'Connell

Salt-stung, rain-cleared air, deepened as always
By a smudge of turf smoke. Overhead the white glide
Of seagulls, and in the convent beeches above the road,
Hoarse croak of rooks, throaty chatter of jackdaws.
High tide pounds stone wall.
I shut the door behind me and head downhill,

Gait steadied by the broad-shouldered gravity
Of houses from the eighteenth or nineteenth century —
Limestone, three storeys, their slate roofs rain-slick,
Aglow with creeper and the green brilliance of mosses.
No force off the Atlantic
Could threaten their angles or budge their masses.

They rise unhurriedly from the strong cellar
And hold a fleshy hand, palm outward, against the sea,
Saying "Land starts here. Go peddle your salt airs elsewhere."
From farms down lanes the meat and milk of pasture,
Root crops and loads of hay,
By hoof or wagon, come down to Kinvara quay.

And so do I — to drink in the presence
Of these presences, these ideas given substance,
Solid as your father's signature
On a letter you unfold sometimes from a quiet drawer,
Yet semi-detached, half free,
Like the road that follows the sea down from Galway,

Curving like a decorated S
Drizzled through a monk's quill plucked from the goose,
Spelling *Sanctus* onto vellum newly missed by the herd,
In a cell where the soul's damp candle flared —
Roofless now to the weather's
Inundations, while ravens walk the cloisters.

Gloria of martyrdom, kingship's crimson
Are shattered now, buried in mire. The mizzling sky
Darkens unmitigated over thatch collapsed in the famine,
Tracks leading nowhere. Absences occupy
The four kingdoms. A wide-eyed
Angel stares uncomprehendingly skyward,

Stone angel of the Island, baptised by rain,
Outlasting Viking longboat, Norman strongbow,
Face battered by a rifle butt. Tough-minded as a bloody saint.
But where was I off to, mind like a darkened window
This dampened afternoon?
To the pub of course. It's time for that quiet pint,

Brewed blacker than ruination, sound
As fresh-hewn timber, strong as a stonecutter's hand.
Make it stout like the roof overhead, to take off the chill
That blows through emptied fields. Let me drink my fill
And more, of that architecture —
Then ease home tight and respectable to dinner.

Abbey Hill

Last season's unpicked blackcurrants clung
To the roadside stonework. Litter papered the hedges,
Jettisoned from passing
Cars. I climbed above the village's
Rooftops and turf smoke; the squared-off wedges
Of Herefords' blunt faces eyed me
With dumb curiosity

As I circled and guessed my way to the place.
The gravel paths were lost and thicketed
In thorn and tea-brown spruce
Ungardened decade after decade.
The gates had been stolen; still the gateposts stood
Toppling, armorial, hierarchic
In the jungling undergrowth.

The house itself loomed finally:
A model of backwater Palladian
Built for fox-hunting gentry
By an English architect from Dublin.
Now just a skeleton. Mist like the undertone
Of a vanished bell hung in an air
No sun or daylight could clear.

I'd seen a marble fireplace-surround
Too grand for the cottage where I'd taken shelter
On a walk once when it rained;
Two Chippendale chairs in a hardware store;
And a dour oil of the Williamite officer
Who stole the land originally,
In the public library.

Seventy years' wet weather had washed
The charred walls clean, but the air held an impression
Of the mad night they smashed
The windows, drunk on restitution
And porter, then jumbled the moveables out on the lawn —
Tall clocks in the garden, books in the trees —
And set Abbey Hill ablaze.

As for the men who torched her, fair play
To them! Their home fires brought down the chandelier,
And the plaster allegory
On the ballroom ceiling crashed to the floor
While the master sat safe in his townhouse in Fitzwilliam Square.
That night's legend grows in the telling,
Famous under thatch of an evening.

But didn't something choice disappear
In that conflagration? An achieved oneness
Of mason and plasterer,
Gardener and host — like the pulse of a timepiece
Flawed and old, or the thought-quickened fineness
Of fingers turning the pages of a book,
Or the daydreams of a girl on horseback?

The Winter Funerals

The postman totters up our street. He's late
Or early, like spring, or he doesn't come at all.
You practice your violin, I'll go for a stroll
And watch the oysterman tarring his boat
That the storm stove in — the rough weather that brought
The lines down that night after New Year's
When the farmers' faces ran with tears
Outside the house where Mary Flatley was laid out.

We've brushed our black clothes off and put them away.
Someone is cooking, someone's out tending the stock
In the grainy drizzle that settles the turf smoke.
Obscured up there in the weathered sky,
The wind that troubled our winter still blows above
The village. We drink it at night with our whiskey
And stir it into our morning tea,
Hearing the tune Charlie played over Maggie's grave.

That drowsy reel's feet danced in the new-dug mud
Of the grave, and held its drained face up to the rain
When he played it slow on his dark accordion —
That grievous dancestep Charlie played.
It follows me out this morning up and down
As I buy a stamp or run an errand
And go for a pint at Flatley's tavern,
Where Mary's smile is nowhere to be seen.

Nowhere in the pipesmoke and mirrored coolness
Where she heard the farmers' chaff with a tolerant ear.
Nowhere to be seen but present everywhere
Amid the slow talk and the Guinness.
Her smile followed the gossip — predictable
As the stuffed pheasants in their glass cases,
Old as the posters for the Galway races.
She gave a love that was almost invisible —

Like the voice at the foot of the garden, the thorny warble
I hear when I get home and pull on my boots
And squelch out among the cabbages and beets
To spot that spring voice, invisible
Or nearly so, that weightless, redbreasted, sparse-feathered
Heartbeat that lilts in the battered garden,
That sings its song for no sound reason
And dies among the thorns unheralded.

You practice your music, I sniff the wind for a sign,
While down in the mud the cabbages glow
With a green persistence. All day you play
That tune, that same old tune, till it's right as rain.

The Ornament

I hated to think of her throwing that old shawl
Over her shoulders and pulling her gumboots on
To venture beneath the lackluster moon,
Stooping out under her low lintel
To search with a weak torch up the Galway road,
Knocking on every cottage door
To ask had they seen her sister,
Who everybody knew was ten years dead.

Fine days, her troubled hair braided and pulled back
Under a crow's-wing hat, she foraged for simples
In the nearby fields or sat in her garden aimless
As weather, watching the robins peck
At breadcrumbs. Shunning the prefab unit
The state provided, she would brew up,
And drink her tea from a delft cup,
At home in the draughty thatch and sunlight.

It was said of her that she came from decent people,
That she married a small farmer, who was dead now.
Her dress, they said, was too fine for a widow,
Her brooch would pay for a funeral —
That knuckled brooch, its tarnished pathos,
Its dimmed emerald a lantern
Lighting a path from the two-room cabin
Back to her childhood's remote half-English house.

I called on the old soul just this Twelfth Night.
She had died two winters back, and whatever
History brought her to those rooms died with her.
I was dragging our Christmas tree out,
Uphill past her house at the top of the village
Where the unpicked blackberries' hulls
Dried on the vines like little skulls —
When I sensed her blue gaze curious over the hedge.

Just a flicker of attention there. On a hunch,
I pushed her door open with my boot, ducked through,
And propped the tree up under the thatchless sky.
Then I placed her brooch on the topmost branch —
That tarnished brooch I took from memory.
It was a gesture of little
Consequence. Not a living soul
Noticed. A crow cawed, and flapped from the chimney.

Rhyme

A pair of aces. The sound of two hands clapping.
A boy sidearms a flat stone, sailing, skipping
It once, twice, four times over the closed surface
Of water, through air's openness.
The sun's vowel roundly springs from the east
Through throaty birdsong in summer
And vast autumnal drowse of color,
To rhyme at day's end frosty in the west.

Pepper and salt. The two it takes to tango.
Yin-yang, Fred & Ginger, John & Yoko.
And you yourself this morning, full-sailed, breeze
Into the room where I write, your blouse
Double-rigged, frankly buttoned, billowy—
As if to say rhymes are matched pairs,
Two swayed and balanced, separate spheres,
Two bell-notes, twin poles of discovery.

Over our garden wall, to the top branch
Of the pear tree blossoming now, a bullfinch
Flies. His honed beak businesslike, his burgher's
Stout midsection splendid, he perches
And preens his pink waistcoat. A model of self-esteem.
Then at his side the female alights,
Jostling the fellow as they take their seats,
Banker and wife at the theatre. That's rhyme.

A History of Windows

At first there were none. Unless you count the bright
Fenestrations of the woodland fringe
Where shaggy hominids hid among the leaves
From predators — or themselves looked hungrily out
At bands of quadrupeds straying into range
Upwind, on unintelligent slow hooves.
Did anyone think then of windows as a medium
Mediating between enclosure and freedom?

Fast-forward a hundred-thousand years or so.
Dowdy monks daydreamed over plainchant and prayer
Through low-set, rounded splays from matins to compline.
Then French-speaking stonemasons arrived from Clairvaux
Chiseling voussoirs that would stand without mortar,
Springing arches toward heaven in airy limestone.
They figured in glass the celestial hierarchy
And dazzled with annunciations the humdrum sky.

The question is whether one would rather
Be looking out or looking in. To stroll
At 2 AM, for instance, on the lawn,
Drink in hand, watching through French doors the other
Revellers boogie down or throw things. Or to loll
In the Georgian library upstairs all afternoon
Reading Trollope, yawning, drinking tea,
Seeing the view the 19th century saw.

Windows and memory. Rain thrown like rice
At the mansard window of a five-franc *pension*.
A student from some unpronounceable place,
I look out over Paris. Windows and rain.
A line-squall rattles our summer-cottage glass.
The children run in, dissolving me back again
To birth-soup, ultimate wetness, broken waters.
I sense light up ahead, and swim toward windows.

Rhymes on the Feast of Stephen

Something has gladdened the blankness of this field,
This rectangle pure as the future, bright as a door
Opened onto snowflakes sharpening the air.
Light-syllabled words, words bewilderingly old
Have printed their inky footfalls here.
I hold the piece of paper to the light
And touch with my fingertips the lodged repose
Of music notched into this whiteness of trees.
I pile up winter fuel in the grate,
Then lean back in my chair and breathe a bit.
Nothing to change: This ink is permanent.
I drink the wassail of vowel and consonant.

An Elegist's Tour of Dublin

Those angels that peer over our shoulders —
Unseen yet vigilant recorders
Of all our myriad percepts and notions,
Dipping quills cut from seraphic pinions
Into ink that will neither fade nor run —
Have they room in their imperishable
Ledgers to transcribe these whimsical
Peregrinations through the streets of Dublin?

Probably not. Our itineraries,
Our eyes that glide through geometries
Of Georgian brick mellowed by northern sun —
They're all slated for demolition.
"There's no preservation society for the likes
Of us," I tell the tweedy, imaginary
Companion who walks with me,
My sight dazzled by plate-glass office blocks.

My companion's a man of my late
Father's generation, composite
Of my more avuncular professors at Harvard —
Acerbic, smokes a pipe, well read
In arcana like *Irish Churches and Monastic
Buildings,* by H. G. Leask, three volumes. "We're all,
I'm sorry to say, Transitional,"
He replies, only north-by-northwest sarcastic.

In the nave of St. Patrick's Cathedral
A doe-eyed Pre-Raphaelite angel
Listens and never bats a glassy eye
As I try to quote three lines from Shelley:
"Life, like a dome of many-colored glass,
Stains the white radiance of Eternity"
And the sun interrupts the Dublin sky
Dappling the limestone and Anglo-Irish brass,

Brightening the day with Victorian pigments.
"Until Death tramples it to fragments,"
My companion closes my quotation and coughs,
Under the sightless eyes of Dean Swift's
Death mask — his indignation hardened to plaster,
His terrifying candor gone gaga,
His days drained to memorabilia,
His breath and his intelligence gone elsewhere.

But where elsewhere does it go — the inner
Cosmos? Does it disappear?
The enormous private store of memory,
The inner maps? My friend and I
Trail off, following our line of vision
Into gravity's blue opposite, which rises
Above the rows of Georgian houses,
Into the ink those recording angels write our lives in.

First Morning Home Again

for Mary

Long sleep. Coffee by noon or thereabouts.
Wild daffodils you gathered blooming to fullness
By the window, open-mouthed and idle as rowboats
Along the quay in the Sunday village stillness.
The most elusive member of the parish,
The transiting, kidglove-colored woodpigeon—
Peaceable, with a saint's name in Irish—
Peregrinates through the fruit trees in our garden,
With a voice like *Columba palumbus*, her name in Latin.

The chaffinch on the stone wall calls "Pink!" "Pink!"
Defying the world to name a different color.
I give the children their presents and unpack,
Closeting two wingtips, a well-fitting pair.
The sight of our folded laundry stacked in a pile,
Fresh-smelling and heterogeneous together
On our bed, gives me an odd little thrill.
The day, luminous and uneventful,
Floats at a cloud's pace through the life we share.

Afternoon at Griffin's

The door out back swings open to a breeze
Off the abandoned burying ground, its names
Destroyed with weather, the stones themselves half gone.
The pub breathes easy. My concentration strays
Over the gardening column in *The Irish Times*.
Voices dip in and out of the slow afternoon —
Rising to a laugh, then slipping back under the surface
Between the practised click of billiards games —
As though time were a very substance, fluid and luminous.

From the bar a measured, systematic clink of coins
Being counted. An immense amount of nothing
Being said. A sigh or two. On the radio the Angelus
Is rung, marking six o'clock, its overtones
Silencing for a moment our talk, then vanishing
In the leaving light. From the window ledge the famous
Stuffed pheasant, our mascot, without assigning blame,
Eyes us with an idiot's vacant intentness.
There's time for another round before starting home.

A Visitation

Why tonight,
   crossing an alien bridge
I should see the faces
   of those two who had died —
damaged moons radiating up
   from the mystery of a river
charging whitely to sea —
   I won't hazard
speculation.
Death is their persuasion, life mine.

One face smashed on the tarmac,
   one face eroded, scabrous,
   delirious on hospital sheets.

Life is the flame that won't singe
anymore
   their danger-prone fingers.

The Way the Petals Fell

The way the petals fell
off the rose I took
(tidying the house we had lived in for a year)
   from Julia's room,
the single rose, overblown, in its brass vase;

the way they landed, on that hideous
   red wall-to-wall shag
carpet in the rented house —
   one, then two discrete petals
   creamy, and fragrant when sniffed

like the cheek of some superannuated aunt
   proffered to be kissed,
   the veined creaminess edged with blush —
those two petals, then four more: six
in all. A pattern: something

   a tealeaf-reader would study
   or a Taoist who augured
from the configuration of prayer beads
tossed ritually onto temple flagstones
   how a day would run.

   It prefigured something —
auspicious I hoped, though
people don't come to me for augury —
   for the journey we were cusping on:
   One sea, one ocean, half a continent.

I gathered the petals (there being
six of us) in the palm of my hand,
  freed the latch on the second-storey casement,
    and released them into the
      August morning:

  you and me
    and our four —
  hostages to gravity, all six.
  I was almost afraid to look —
    superstition I suppose —
      as they navigated the air.

A Backward Glance at Galway

for Thomas Lynch

I can almost predict what it would be like
If I should ever go back: The medieval
Streets aswarm with German tourists in Aran
Sweaters, piling off coaches, in town for Race Week;
I'd be craning up at the facade of Lynch's Castle
Studying an anachronistic bartizan,
Getting jostled and elbowed and breathed on by every
Member of the European Community.

But I had my innings there, hitching the coast road
Through salt meadows saturated and green,
Then walking up from the quays—a wind at my back
With the North Atlantic behind it, that thinned the coalsmoke
And refreshed with raindrops the chiseled limestone.
I would hole up in Naughton's pub with my notebook
Ferreting words from a secondhand thesaurus,
Sounding out rhymes in a snug with a pint of Guinness.

From those raptures all I have to show is a snapshot
That I took last December from Nuns' Island
Of the crumbling city walls and quayside quarter.
In the frosty air the slate roofs show up white,
The chimney-pots sooty and Dickensian.
The river pushes downstream glistening with power.
And nothing stands between the lens and the sky
But clarity and salt and a breeze off the sea.

Passage

for Joshua, Julia, Andrew and Charles

> "The use of travelling is to regulate imagination by
> reality, and instead of thinking how things may be,
> to see them as they are."
>> — Dr. Johnson

I would gather you — asleep, or pretending sleep —
From your beds and snug you into the Volkswagen
Or later the red boatlike Country Squire,
And we'd be low-gearing up the western slope
Of the Rockies before you woke again
To breakfast and the dazzling snows of departure.
It was too early yet to quote Dr. Johnson
Or to speak of travel as a metaphor.

Perhaps I should wish you to live "like some green laurel
Rooted in one dear perpetual place"
As Yeats wished. But then I would miss seeing you learn
The abrupt scene-changes and fresh starts of travel,
Waking this morning in our borrowed Highgate house
Hearing the remote shuttle of an outbound train,
With a sea, an ocean, half a hemisphere
Between ourselves and all that's familiar.

Infatuated may you walk beside the Seine
And steam along the Grand Canal in a vaporetto
(Gondolas being too costly). Then acquire
Farsi on the silk route through Afghanistan,
Or swot up something really hard like Pushtu
And bargain for turquoise in a mountain bazaar
Think of me as you bathe in the ashy Ganges
And the Himalayas first whiten your dazzled eyes.

May you study maps, count suitcases, always remember
What pockets you keep things of value in.
The self exists on the far side of a border;
First crossings can seem a trifle strange.
May travellers' luck go with you when you pay your coin
Of passage over that last, unbridgeable river,
Reckoning on practiced fingers the rate of exchange,
Speaking the deathless argot of your boatman.

House with Children

First the white cat named after Indians
Slipped in — too fat by half,
White marked with five black spots like sudden stones
In the snow — poked in through his hidden door,
Set flowing through the house a draft,
A chill tangled in the winter of his fur.

Alerted to those skulks, those leaps, those claws,
The sparkless energy-efficient
Furnace fired, pouring warmth through every vent
Of the house's two-storey stucco repose.

Julia slept her seven summers' worth
On a cloud of goose down, hugged by cushioned paws,
Dreaming. The wind blew out of the north.
Josh sprawled among paper fantasies.
Even Andrew rested from his wonderings,
His pages of lion, witch, and so forth.
Their three doors swayed in the warm domestic breeze
As Iroquois strolled past in his wanderings.

Drawn, was it, by the fragrance of marriage, he leapt
To the bed where the man woke and the woman slept
And the three-years' life between them burned fitfully
In a moment of fever, then woke laughing soundlessly.

Charles woke, and cooled his hands on the cat's chill fur.
In the clock's dimness white and dark spots blended.
The mercury stuck high, snow hung suspended
Like a V of geese over Canada.
The house and its people lodged secure
That night. Snow fell nowhere but Narnia.
There at the back of the wardrobe a door
Between the deep cold and the greatcoats stood ajar.

Convergence

You knew it was there, you could sense it
Greenly inherent in the wood
Through dull months when you didn't notice
Life fattening in the bud.
Now April fulfills itself with whitethorn,
And lilacs overarched with birdsong.

A lash under the lid, the suspicion
Of pain in the third molar, a flicker's
Speckled flutter into fieldglasses'
Pursuing circle of focus.
The E-string twists, retrieving, past sharp and flat,
Then sounds the sought-for, in-tune note.

The glow of a summer's day breathing
Off a river at nightfall. Cutlery's faint
Clatter on summer-cottage china
Up-ridge. You cast to a hint
Of trout in a pool. A violent, muscled swirl
And the hard jaw clamps the feathered steel.

What trick of the night's is it, that you wake
Chilled and alert, fingering
A soreness, picturing cells
Gone rife and hungering —
That you know, as the doctor nods you politely
In, what news he has to give you?

Twos

The rooms where you entertained me are open to view
And expensive now. But I'm drawn that way.

The sea steps ashore up wide ascents of marble.
Corinthian columns ruffle like bedclothes.

Rough side of a towel, smooth side of silk.
Your mare's-tails unravel, and cloud the royal blue.

A brown Raleigh three-speed. A wide-tired Schwinn.
Bricks glow, air whirls, horizon wheels up grey.

I leaf into a lane, thirsting for cloudburst.
You're wet, like a gardenia.

I speak bright plumage.
Your breeze blows in.

Table

from the Turkish of Edip Cansever

A man filled with the gladness of living
Put his keys on the table,
Put flowers in a copper bowl there.
He put his eggs and milk on the table.
He put there the light that came in through the window,
Sound of a bicycle, sound of a spinning wheel.
The softness of bread and weather he put there.
On the table the man put
Things that happened in his mind.
What he wanted to do in life,
He put that there.
Those he loved, those he didn't love,
The man put them on the table too.
Three times three make nine:
The man put nine on the table.
He was next to the window next to the sky;
He reached out and placed on the table endlessness.
So many days he had wanted to drink a beer!
He put on the table the pouring of that beer.
He placed there his sleep and his wakefulness;
His hunger and his fullness he placed there.
Now that's what I call a table!
It didn't complain at all about the load.
It wobbled once or twice, then stood firm.
The man kept piling things on.

Osman's Dream

A tree sprang from his navel, and its shade
Encompassed the world — the known world, or all the known
World worth knowing about. Where the dream tree spread
Its beneficent shade and influence, a mountain
Asserted itself, snow-crowned through Olympian cloud.
(Though the Turk was master under heaven,
Didn't the sybarite Greek deities
Still lounge in the clouds with their nectar and their boys?)

Snowmelt quickened, and annunciated down slopes;
Water circumambulated the mountain.
Men drank it and fished it and watered purple grapes;
The air freshened with musk of the Persian melon.
Rough cavalry from grass-poor northern steppes
Pastured their ponies and bathed in a marble fountain.
They washed from their feet a continent's dust
And scrubbed from their Asian hands the blood of conquest.

The crushed petals of a summer's roses, Osman
Dreamed. The black tincture from beetles' husks;
And a blue distilled from the sky at noon.
A hand steady as an archer's dipped a paintbrush
And painted the names of God — all ninety-nine
Of them — across the walls of the royal mosque.
Osman stirred in his tent, awakened
By the crunch of his bodyguards' spurred boots in the sand.

Then slept again, and prayed in the mosque of his dream:
The Sultan, the "Shadow of God on Earth." Merchants
Rolled out their carpets in the atrium,
Bazaar streets honeycombed from the mosque precincts,
Selling the sanctity of Byzantium —
While foot soldiers with unplaceable accents
Fluted the women of the Christians
And trampled the as-yet unflowering gardens.

The Night of Displacement

from the Turkish of Sezaî Karakoc

1.

The moon cut-off, the road like a rope tonight,
The evening's dishes contaminated with death.
Then like a thousand years' rain falling all at once
A leaf tore from the Book of the Law.

Tonight a peerless wall collapsed.
Here and there wind-devils sprang up.
The crowing of a silvered cock, the moon
Descending to earth like a green leaf.

Tonight I did apprentice work.
Through the rain that separates, the fire that melds,
I calibrated souls into the sky.
In the night I became an eye, a morning's freshness.

2.

Tonight as if in a flash their graves
Split in two, the dead abandoned the city
Like a snowball in front of a fire,
Like the air escaping from a tire.

May there not remain even a single soul
Underground in the city this oppressive night!
The dead themselves, thinned and made light,
Seem cities poised to fly.

The moon cut-off, I am a stalwart grave-dissolver,
A flawless and unstirred pitcher replenishing the nights.
Earth's fugitives, the emptied shells of the dead,
Congregate in the doors and gardens of the mosques.

Pasha's Daughter, 1914

for James Stewart-Robinson

Braided into a single complication
Down the back of her nightdress, her hair shows grey
As pearls and white as a cloud as she steps coldly
To open the curtains' plum velvet, stiff with thread of silver,
Onto a sky above Istanbul. Mehmet brings *chai*
On a silver tray worn through to copper.

A Jerusalem cypress in her garden
That arrows the sky as a minaret does —
Its lines liquid as a page of Persian —
A leaded mosque-dome full and silvery in the pause
Between showers, give her the sense of having awakened
And been served tea in Paradise.

Paradise is a bedraggled trapezoid
Of outback, its fountain a brew of leaves,
Its marble paths dog-fouled. The Black Sea wind blows
Trash against untended tulips gone to seed.
Rain storms and gutters down the overarching eaves
And rattles the quiet of her windows.

Tarnished stars invisible above Istanbul
Govern, while trains from Aleppo and the Balkans
Shuttle broken armies home to the capital.
The ground buckles under tombstones. Marble turbans
Crack, as the bones of the ancients are shoveled aside
To make space for the freshly dead.

Mehmet comes in again, six centuries
Of marches and conquests reduced to the dirt
On his cuffs. Moustache dispirited, nomadic cheekbones
Wintry, he lights a fire, smudging the famous skies
With coal scavenged from the cobbled street.
Her eyes would break bones.

Thunder now — like the clatter of musketry,
Like war ponies galloped across borders,
Like bronze siege-cannon pounding Viennese stone,
Like the voice of a shattered gong the circumference of the sky.
"Bring opium to me by the window," she orders,
"While I watch our empire melt in the rain."

Southbound Pullman, 1945

Discharge papers in duffel bags,
Their train thumps half-speed out of Boston.
Sunset kindles the cokey haze
Over Back Bay Station.

Bricky courtyards, windswept corners and
Clotheslines, a view of someone's kitchen.
A Victory garden with fists of cabbage.
Then the lights switch on.

A boy and his father burning leaves,
Obscured by dusk on a patch of green,
Wave up at faces starred in the southbound's
Passing constellation.

Stewards uncork bottles, ice clinks
In the club car. A new deck
Crackles. Atlantic sea-salt blows in,
And a whiff of coalsmoke.

Steam builds. The whistle finds its pitch
And sounds an airy, unstopped note
Over darkling marshes and shore towns
Shutting down for the night.

Dinner is gonged through aisles of opened
Collars and bourbon. The galley
Vents coffee-scald and steak-sizzle
Down the Connecticut valley.

Penn Station at midnight. Bustle of redcaps,
Morning editions, hot java, trainmen
Tuning the wheels with big wrenches.
Then distances again.

Porterly hands tuck ironed cotton
And turn drowsy blankets back.
Darkness cradles the swaying coaches
Over strumming track.

Snoring. Then a nightmare scream
Jangles to its feet the whole sleeper.
Home voices murmur "You're okay, son."
"The war's over, soldier."

All night the breathing of ploughed fields.
The continent opens like a hand.
Tomorrow, bands and a convertible.
Then fresh mistakes begin.

Allen's Station: They

for Beverly Travers

The stars cool their fires in the river of night.

The big people sleep.
I step out barefooted onto the dewy, rough-boarded porch
And open my eyes among farm buildings.
Their yellow pine boards and whitewash
Illuminate my way.

Down the kitchen-garden path, through the orchard,
All the way this side of the leaning barn
Where the horses shuffle and snore,
Past a slumbering bull in a meadow,
Past the for-once quiet chickens

I pad over velvet dust,
Through heady stands of ragweed,
Past the cooks' cabin
Where Kate and Aunt Martha
Have lit the morning lamp already
In their sturdy square cabin
Wallpapered with years of the Sunday comics.

Orphan Annie's eyes
Never narrow or squint
Like Aunt Martha's do
And Dick Tracy is forever in profile
And will never look straight at lame, hobbled Martha
Who was born a slave
And because even her church is on the property,
Has never left these acres.

And red-headed, Cherokee Kate
Who never has a civil word for *no one*
But my Uncle Frank — Why is that, I wonder? —
A different kind of uncle;
A cousin more like, if the tree were drawn.

Dagwood blunders across these walls
And will do so in his Bumstead way
Until the paper peels.

And Blondie with her thirties frizz
Is out shopping again
And will again commit the crime of unthrift;
And Major Hoople in his quilted dressing-gown harrumphs,
Fires up his meerschaum pipe
And sums up his opinion of life at Allen's Station:
"Egad!"

George A. and his wife and her sister and her sister's husband
And their three children, and Napoleon,
And a walleyed Indian-looking woman with a corncob pipe,
And some people I don't recognize
Are going to the fields today to chop cotton.

Their blue overalls bleached to the ghost of white,
Their streaming Mason jars of well water,
Their readiness for whatever reason to work twelve hours
In the West Tennessee sun —
People today don't look like them, or talk like them.

The whites of Napoleon's eyes are purple.
Later in the morning, when he feels a little better,
He'll tell me again about the penitentiary
And show me the healed, pink bullet hole in his arm.

I'm seven, the farmer's little cousin from Memphis.

The lug-wheeled John Deere tractor
Strains with its wagonload of people
And follows the sun up and over the raised L & N tracks
That divide our farm from Beverly's father's.

The land surrounds us with its life:
Not the soil only — the oaks and poplars and sycamores
And cotton plants and birds and beasts,
And all of us a part of it:
The people who work it, the farmer who owns it,
The boy who watches.

At the end of August my uncle
Will flag down the L & N
And I'll ride it to Memphis
Through the whitewashed towns and sparse farms
And be met in a car
At the big station built with cotton dollars,
And go back to school
And grow up and move away.

They stay in the fields.
I watch them chop cotton,
Drinking water from their jar —
And them not seeming to mind —

As the dense green cotton leaves burn
And the purple boll explodes into ripeness
And the sun describes its slow arc.

They chop cotton, and stay right where they are.

Firstness

Early pleasures please best, some old voice whispers:
Cozy holdings, the heart's iambic thud
And sly wanderings — lip-touchings, long summers,
The rain's pourings and pipings heard from bed;
Earth-smell of old houses, airy ceilings,
A boy's brainy and indolent imaginings.

Twenty years gone then that boy is gone,
Speeding down beach roads in a friend's MG.
Love, or the limey buzz of a g 'n' t —
Or better, both — and the watery hunter's moon,
Accelerate the engines of the night,
And set a long chase afoot.

Today, twenty years older than that even,
I breathe quietness and fresh-laundered linen,
Kneeling, seeing with eyes opened white brick,
Smelling Sunday, mumbling beside my son those words
About a lost sheep, and someone's having erred.
Thank God for instinct, and beginner's luck.

Five Sketches, Winter

1.

Bedraggled quadrangle.

A stone sill, chisel-marked.
The snow arranges, flake by flake,
itself over the stone.

2.

The gloom of trees
is a Chinese pistol
Pollocked in ink-black shots.

3.

Old copper,
moss-green under shifting white.
Down a steep roof
snow slides.

4.

Vinyl-topped café tables,
one silvery with melting snow,
one still a white loaf

with borders of run.

5.

First snow, then freezing rain.
Down plate glass, a long rattail of drip.

Another plate of cabbage and potatoes, please.

Two Sketches, Summer

1.

Ice cubes thrown into tall grass.
Voices way out in a meadow.
Red caviar spilled on a black Lab.

2.

A little green thing, a bug,
delicate, composed—
six legs, two orange antennae,
gazelle-like—
lands on a potato chip.

Camp Shadywillow

A June breeze flutters across the meadow
Like a slow curve, like the last day of school,
Like a love letter — like the trees standing still,
Never moving their feet in or out of the shadow
At Camp Shadywillow.

The pine-needled sunlight filtering down
Through the lacy brim of an old fishing hat,
A song with good words, that goes on and on,
And a reggae guitar-lick — *I like it like that!*

You might happen to see, at Camp Shadywillow,
A bandanna-haired, earringed, thin-chested fellow
With a Chinese beard and a habit of braggin'
Changing the tire on an orange Volkswagen.

And a lady called Shakti, I tell you she's *built.*
When she starts to party, she parties full tilt.
She smells like patchouli, she's made like a cello —
One look and you feel like you've smoked half a kilo
At Camp Shadywillow.

They'll roll you some homegrown, they'll pour you some wine.
You'll be glad you drove over from New Lebanon
For occult conversation and gooseberry fool.
The sky there's as blue as God's swimming pool.

As blue as the silk of Kubla Khan's pillow
When he goes for his afternoon opium nap
At his rural retreat out back of Fox Hollow
Just a few miles from Stockbridge (it's not on the map).

He's not dreaming of bridge, or croquet, or fine wine
From the cellars of Ernest and Julio Gallo,
Nor his newly appointed court concubine
With her passionate eyes and her mystical halo —
He's dreaming of two weeks at Camp Shadywillow.

On a Gothic Ivory

for James Boyd White

What calculations leapt forward in his mind
As he hefted the tusk, an elongated crescent
Moon, and showed the carpenter the piece
He wanted sawed, brushing the snow off with his hand,
Having given to the carpenter's wife as a present
The cloth it had come wrapped in, to make a dress —
As he planned his winter, and rocked back on his heels
Absorbing the pure light off snowy foothills
Through eyes sharpened by habitual dimness,

By early dawnings half-glimpsed through darkened splays,
Ink ground in silence, mixed with rainwater —
That's a knowledge to which I am not privy.
Summoned and fetched down stone passageways,
Through the slype, along the north range of the cloister,
He stood out now in the courtyard of the monastery
Watching lay monks unload salt and treasure,
Bags of spices, discreet ingots of silver,
Tools sent from Damascus by the duke's emissary.

The carver of ivory, asked to affirm the Creed —
I believe in one God, the Father Almighty,
Maker of heaven and earth. And of all things seen
And unseen — would not I think have qualified
Those words edged with snowy clarity
As you or I might: *Well, yes, but not what you mean*
By "God," and not in the usual sense of "believe,"
And not, I rather suspect, what you might have
In mind when you say "I." He was a plainer man.

But rendering the stun of the Crucifixion,
God's only son murdered, the carver felt
Awkward and ashamed, as though he intruded himself
Onto an action too human for depiction,
Too mired in flesh for the eyes of devotion, except
As the discovery of a geometrical moment:
The right crucified arm lining up in his composition
With the Mother of God drying a tear stage-left
On the ivory hem of her Byzantine garment.

I feel the carving lighten and clarify
Once he has done justice to the holy scene
And is free to ascend into perpendiculars,
Which parallel minute cracks in the ivory.
My eye homes in on the circular medallion —
A sunburst cross couched in a circle — that centers
Itself at the nexus of the cross Christ hangs on:
A touch that thinks forward to Bernini's throne
In the southward and worldly dazzle of St. Peter's.

Here, though, we are provincial and northern, far
From proportion and the noonday sun. Above the surround
Of shame and crossed hopes where hooded figures offer
Him gall to drink and a soldier jabs his spear
Between God's ribs, an arch like one I found
Behind a hay barn in Burgundy one summer
Raises its shelter — pointed, and shady underneath.
You can hear the builders catch their breath
As the scaffolding comes down, and each voussoir

Settles into position, snug as every
Belled hour of the canonical day. But this is no church —
Though it looks like one — with stained glass and spires
And human error. It's a hand-sized slab of ivory.
The angle and in-drawn breath of its dominant arch
Will not sag or weaken. After six hundred years
Nothing can fade the aura of the carver's sweat
And concentration, the chrism of candlelight
And sanctuary that have seeped into its pores.

Objects

He would have wrapped a coarse cloth I imagine
About the icon, taking with him the Virgin's
Gaze of power, her countenance blackened
By dim centuries of candle-blur and worry —
Tucking it away in his saddlebag.
You can see a crease here where the frame was scored
With wire.
                              A dim foreknowledge of the road's
Rutted mire and snowdrifts would have shivered
Through his plans as he heard the loud sycamore
Leaves skitter, desiccated, across the bricked
Herringbone of the cloister's footpaths.

Then a winey ambuscade of espaliered
Quinces, overripe and unpicked, whets
His sense of loss, the abbey deserted now,
The *ghazis'* bronze mortars thudding closer
Among chestnut trees the order planted
Along their eastern ridges.
                                        He tenders
Between his hands, before stowing it, the chalice —
Cupping it in his palms the way you hold
A face from your youth, thumbing its silver bowl
Like the cheekbones of the Blessed Virgin.

The hunting glide of a peregrine falcon slices
Through his hesitation. He fumbles the sign of the cross,
Shuts the oak door with a thud behind him,
Then locks it with his medieval key.

And thinking that if God wills, the Emperor's troops
Might fight their way back into these mountains
By spring, he throws the key into a snowdrift
And mounts.

Aerogramme

Afoot, at large in these streets again —
relict not of the city's old grandeur
but wandering where my own errant
days once wandered off to. Where a woman
in on-again off-again blowsy weather
having sent the children off on some errand,
fingered with rainy fingertips her curtain

idly, to gaze out over the years —
her hair springy from dampnesses —
then opened her currents to mine.
Eighteen years give or take, since fireflied by stars
one night under cypresses our impulses
first brushed together and began
the navigated muscular migration

upstream, lifelong.
Today she's an ocean
and half a continent absent.
But her slow airs reach
me, leaving me wondering, and past wondering, why the rain
seamlessly layering speaks green in her accent,
transfiguring my old touch
of starry fingers that swam her nubbly rush,

the hand that angles this pen. The years
speckle it like a trout. At night
my dreams glide beside her. Awake
I'm heraldic stonework refreshed by showers,
transparent on my feet as a walking spirit.
I breathe her in like the smoke
of my days, the rain-quickened updraft from home-fires.

Transport

for Mary

Great Plains Lakotas breaking camp in winter.
The light contrivance they have fashioned
From horsehide torn into inch-wide strips, cross-woven
On a frame of saplings — this springy carrier
Harnessed to a pony, who gentles a sick woman
Through Dakota snows. In Donegal a farmer
Hauls the same idea with mules up a rocky slope,
Loaded with turf for the cottage fire.
There's a name for this conveyance: a "slype."

Wheels next. Boards sawed from crude-hewn hickory
Nailed together into a square,
Roughed off into a circle. An idea flares
In the grey dawn of technology!
The notion of carriage evolves, and the farmer
Has got himself a cart, then a trap, then a landau.
Picture these notions in a Platonic museum
Of transport: slype, then cart, then tractor;
A coach-and-four by a Pontiac Trans-Am.

And so on. Likewise I, though at first as dumb
As any boy, and as diffident,
Have been transported in vehicles I hadn't
The imagination to posit, and at first never dreamed
Of intensities beyond the moment
I might be carried to — where a woman's plummy
Thighs opened to a salty
Updraft of quickened wings flying home
To an unvisited interior. This was poetry.

Which brings me to the moving truck I saw
Drive through a thundercloud of pollution
In Athens one diesel-darkened afternoon
While over the traffic floated the white geometry
Of the Parthenon. In Greek letters the sign
Read μεταφορα, like an epiphany
(Greek word and Greek idea itself) —
As if the angel of my education
Had emblazoned it there through the smog on my behalf.

Metaphor, then. The transport of something or someone
From anywhere to somewhere else.
And haven't I translated my fickle pulse,
My pints of blood, my nervous system and brain
This distance, for reasons that don't amount to much?
Only to find myself, over longitudes, drawn
Back in thought to your bed, to the lovely curve
Of your pleasure, my chief preoccupation
And delight — without which the poem would not live,

No imprint would be made on the featureless blur,
No destination, only distance.
Nor this morning would the rain's splash and spatter
Onto airport glass transfigure
Into your voice, your emblem and presence —
Fetching me back through a slipstream of allure
With travelled eyes and the released hands of a captive,
Steering by dark stars of absence
Homeward, to take up again where we left off.

Bearings

Saturated dazzle of jonquils,
Precipitous drenched limestone outcroppings
Where I wandered lonely as
Only a boy such as myself
Could, it seemed, be.

Dense turnings of a midcity park
Honeysuckle-tangled, down paths I bumped along —
The only boy in Memphis
Thinking at that moment of Herrick —
Astraddle a directionless bike.

How did I come by the gifted indolence
Of Saturday mornings when I slept and woke
To remote soundings of foghorns
From riverboats that channeled their way
Through an atmosphere as thick

As the whiteness that seizes the March skies
In this north my turnings have brought me to? —
In a bright cafe anonymous,
Wanting nothing more than to lose myself
And free the drift of my compass.

Span

Childhood
of the boy I was
fell light, like a snowflake,

depositing a red fleck
for every wrong sustained,
in the russet of my pupiled eyes.

In the overarching blue,
nascent whorls
of condensation

imprint themselves
and dissolve.

A book opens, it closes.

ABOUT THE AUTHOR

RICHARD TILLINGHAST is the author of five books of poetry, including *Sleep Watch* (1969), *The Knife and Other Poems* (1980), and *Our Flag Was Still There* (1984), as well as the forthcoming critical memoir *Robert Lowell: Damaged Grandeur*. Born in 1940 in Memphis, Tennessee, Tillinghast was educated at Sewanee and at Harvard. Since 1983 he has been on the faculty of the University of Michigan, where he is a Professor of English and teaches in the Master of Fine Arts program. He has received grants from the National Endowment for the Humanities, the Woodrow Wilson Foundation, the Amy Lowell Trust, the British Council, and the American Research Institute in Turkey. His book reviews and literary essays have appeared in various periodicals, including *The New York Times Book Review, Washington Post Book World, The New Criterion, Partisan Review,* and *The New York Times* Sunday Travel Section, for which he writes regularly. Richard Tillinghast is married and is the father of a daughter and three sons.

THE STONECUTTER'S HAND
was set in eleven point Adobe Garamond, a
revival of the famous Garamond typefaces
that were based on recastings of sixteenth-
century designer Claude Garamond's origi-
nal metal versions. The Adobe version was
designed by Rob Slimbach of Adobe Systems.